Legit

The Rise of a Cyber Athlete

By Ron Berman

www.av2books.com

Your AV² Media Enhanced book gives you an online audio book, and a self-assessment activity. Log on to www.av2books.com and enter the unique book code from this page to access these special features.

Go to **www.av2books.com**, and enter this book's unique code.

BOOK CODE

J898746

AV² by Weigl brings you media enhanced books that support active learning.

AV² Audio Chapter Book Navigation

HIGHLIGHTED TEXT   ACTIVITIES   HOME   CLOSE

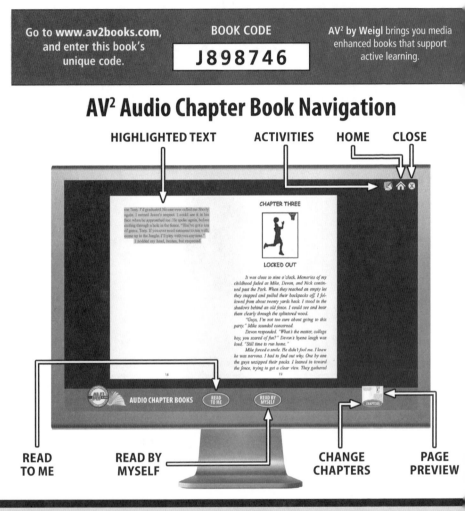

READ TO ME   READ BY MYSELF   CHANGE CHAPTERS   PAGE PREVIEW

Published by AV² by Weigl
350 5th Avenue, 59th Floor
New York, NY 10118

Website: www.av2books.com   www.weigl.com

First Published by Scobre Educational Press.

Library of Congress Control Number: 2013937475
ISBN 978-1-62127-983-9 (hardcover)
ISBN 978-1-62127-939-6 (single-user eBook)
ISBN 978-1-48960-014-1 (multi-user eBook)

Printed in the United States of America in North Mankato, Minnesota
1 2 3 4 5 6 7 8 9 0   17 16 15 14 13

062013
WEP310513

TABLE OF CONTENTS

Gaming is one of the fastest growing sports in America. Check out the exciting action at a recent professional tournament.

Chapter One

Cyber Athletes

Nobody can deny that the world is changing. This is especially true when it comes to sports and competition. Sure, in countries like Italy and Brazil, a classic sport like soccer still rules. In America, baseball players dream of the World Series, while football players hope to play on Super Bowl Sunday.

These days, there are new sports to enjoy as well. The X Games is a good example. Skateboarding and snowboarding are becoming as popular as any mainstream sport. And now, technology is changing everything. Sports now take place far beyond skate parks and mountain tops. Athletes are competing in cyberspace.

These athletes are called "cyber athletes." They love playing video games, but not just for fun. They are professionals, like pro athletes in other sports. The NBA has LeBron James, who is one of the greatest basketball players in the world. There are cyber athletes who are just as good at what *they* do.

So, what is a cyber athlete? He or she is someone who plays video games in tournaments. Cyber athletes come in all shapes, sizes, and ages. They practice hard and compete against other gamers. The very best of them join pro leagues—and some of them earn a *lot* of money.

The rise of the cyber athlete has happened pretty recently. In 2001, the first World Cyber Games were held in South Korea. Famous cyber athletes from around the world showed up to compete. They wanted to win the tournament and become known as the world's best "cyber warrior." They also wanted a piece of the $300,000 being awarded in prize money.

Video games are a lot of fun. For some cyber athletes, though, it's like Puff Daddy said: "It's all about the Benjamins!"

There wouldn't be any cyber athletes if there were no cyberspace itself. The Internet connects the world. It gives us music, movies, games, shopping, and information. More importantly, the Internet puts you in touch with people. Close to 1 billion people surf the Web every day! They communicate instantly through cyberspace. Have you ever stopped to consider how amazing that is? Can you even imagine the world your parents grew up in—a world where people were *not* connected?

We are living in a time of great progress. Especially in the field of communications technology. We take much of it for granted, but we really shouldn't. Imagine how different things would be if Alexander Graham Bell hadn't invented the telephone. Bell's invention connected people over distances far greater than they could have ever dreamed. That concept has led to much of the technology that is part of our daily lives. This includes the Internet, cell phones, and even live gaming. Imagine the look on Mr. Bell's face if he were able to witness two people playing Xbox—one player in California and the other one in New York!

The world has changed because of technology and the Internet. Young people understand this very well, sometimes even better than adults. In fact, 12 to 18-year-olds like to be the first ones to check out new technology. Teenagers carried MP3 players while their parents were still listening to CDs. They were also the first ones to send text messages and use digital cameras. They even learned how to shoot video directly from their cell phones.

In some cases, young people are the ones *creating* new technology. You may have heard the story of Larry Page and Sergey Brin. Back in the 1990s, they were college students. They started working together to develop a new search engine for the Internet. What did they come up with? Google, which is now used by millions of people every day.

Understanding technology is a good thing for young people. It's cool, and it can also lead to career opportunities. Chad Hurley and Steve Chen are good examples. These two friends wanted to watch videos on the Internet. They were frustrated by how difficult it was. So they came up with an idea that would make it easier and more enjoyable. Their idea became known as YouTube. Before long, it was one of the most popular Web sites on the Net.

It's obvious that thousands of new career opportunities are popping up. As with Google or YouTube, technology is *big* business. Billions of dollars are being spent on research, software, and many other things. Microsoft spends over $5 billion a year just on research and development!

Young people are discovering that they can have exciting careers in fields that interest them. Some of these jobs are in the video game industry (which is also referred to as "interactive entertainment"). Sure, it's fun to kick back and play video games. And for those who are really talented, competing professionally is an option. It can also be rewarding to work for a software company. For example, you can be part of a team that develops and sells video games. Not only is it fun, but it's also a way to earn a fantastic living.

The idea of making money in the video game industry is fairly new. It would have been impossible just a few years ago. There are now thousands of people getting involved. They get paid to help create and sell the games they love to play!

It's incredible that everything came together so quickly. It may have been because of the World Cyber Games and other tournaments. They were very successful. As a result, video game leagues were created.

In 2002, the first professional video game league was born in the United States. It was known as Major League Gaming (MLG). The league focuses on console video games (not computer games). Some of the best professional gamers in the country play in MLG.

MLG holds live competitions all across America. These are opportunities for gamers to become well known. One of the brightest young MLG pros is 16-year-old Bryan Rizzo of Palm Harbor, Florida. Bryan travels around the country playing *Halo 2*.

When he's home, Bryan can usually be found in his room. He will be staring at his flat-screen TV, with an Xbox controller in hand. He wears a headset, which connects him to his teammates. They talk about upcoming tournaments, discuss strategy, and have fun messing around. Mostly though, they practice hard. Sometimes they spend several hours a night getting ready for the next tournament.

At only 16, Bryan is one of MLG's top players. That's quite an achievement, considering the tough competition. It shows how determined he is. Bryan hadn't planned to become a professional gamer. It's awesome that it worked out that way, though. His success has led to some great rewards. He's had the opportunity to travel and earn money. He's also made lifelong friends and learned a lot about the video game business.

Bryan's journey began more than six years ago. At that time he was an average 10-year-old kid. Like his friends, he had already been into video games for a long time. Compared to most people he knew, gaming came pretty easily to Bryan. He played whenever he had free time, usually between school and baseball practice.

Nobody could have predicted that one day Bryan would be a famous gamer. *He* certainly never expected to travel around the country as one of MLG's top stars. One thing was sure, though—when it came to video games, Bryan was a natural.

Chapter Two

Legit

"As far back as I can remember, I dreamed of being a pro baseball player," says Bryan. He smiles as he tries on his old third baseman's glove. This statement seems strange coming from a professional cyber athlete. But it's true. Bryan Rizzo's childhood was *not* all about gaming. Growing up in sunny Florida, life was about being outdoors. There was swimming, street hockey, and his first love—baseball.

Bryan's interest in baseball goes back many years. His father was an excellent player himself.

Mr. Rizzo was actually drafted by a Major League team back in 1981 (the Kansas City Royals). He had many great experiences in his baseball career and made a lot of friends. In fact, one of his buddies was his teammate, David Cone. A talented pitcher, Cone won the American League Cy Young Award in 1994.

During Bryan's childhood, Mr. Rizzo spent a lot of time outside with Bryan and his older brother, Tyler. He would give them tips on hitting and fielding. Bryan also has memories of trips with his family to watch Major League Baseball games. Nothing was more fun than actually playing, though. He spent many long summer days enjoying his favorite sport.

Bryan at the plate.

As time went on, Bryan's interest shifted to gaming. In the early days, Bryan and Tyler played computer games as often as video games. Among other favorites, they were really into sports games. They liked *John Madden Football* and *Major League Baseball*, both from EA Sports.

A few years later, they got a Sega Genesis. It was their first gaming system. Bryan's choice of games was *Sonic the Hedgehog*. This game took players on an adventure with a hedgehog named Sonic. Their Sega Genesis was eventually replaced by a Nintendo 64, and Bryan moved on to games such as *Starfox* and *James Bond*. He was around 9 years old at the time.

The making of a video game champion: the early days.

That was just the beginning. Something big happened a couple of years later. Bryan was almost 12 at the time, but he remembers it like it was yesterday. His parents bought an Xbox for him and Tyler. The system had better graphics and improved gameplay. It was a huge upgrade over the Nintendo 64.

The first game Bryan played on Xbox was the original *Halo*. That was back in 2002. At the time, Bryan was just an average sixth grader who loved baseball. But all of a sudden, he became totally involved in the amazing world of *Halo*.

This time period also marked the beginning of a change in Bryan's life. Over the next three years, his family moved around a lot. By the time Bryan was a ninth grader in 2005, he had moved several times. He went to different schools and lived in houses in both Florida and Tennessee.

Moving around was difficult. Still, Bryan adjusted well to every new situation. His life had always centered on school and baseball. By the time his family settled back in Florida for good, Bryan's interest in video games was even greater. They were beginning to play a larger role in his daily activities.

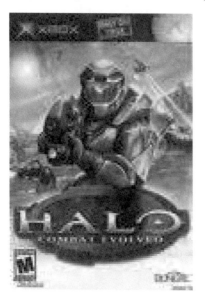

As Bryan became more involved with *Halo*, he stopped playing almost all other video games. Obviously he wasn't a pro in the very beginning. *Halo* was simply a game he played for fun. But something special was happening every time Bryan picked up his Xbox controller. He felt comfortable in the three- dimensional cyber world that he viewed on the screen. Sometimes he almost felt as if he were inside the game himself.

Bryan had always enjoyed playing video games with his friends. But when it came to *Halo*, he was way out of their league. Although Bryan is a modest guy, he admits it. "Yeah, I was the best player among my friends," he says. "I always ended up getting the most kills. At first, I figured I just had a good feel for the game. Eventually, though, I started to think that maybe it was more than that."

Like millions of *Halo* fans, Bryan remembers the excitement surrounding *Halo 2*. Everyone was waiting for it to be released. At the time, Bryan was a freshman at Countryside High, in Clearwater, Florida. He was training for the upcoming baseball season. When *Halo 2* was released, Bryan's priorities changed completely.

There was a very good reason for all the hype about *Halo 2*. Up until then, *Halo* was played mainly against the computer. It could also be played with friends who were in the same room. *Halo 2* offered a new twist. It was called Xbox Live—an online gaming service. People could now match up against opponents across town. They could even play against people in a different city, state, or country. The world of interactive entertainment had gone live.

Online gaming didn't start with Xbox Live, of course. It had been around for many years. But Xbox Live was new, easy to use, and awesome. Users would pay a small monthly fee. Then they could connect with other Xbox Live players through the Internet. It was a lot more fun than sitting around and playing against the computer. During this period of time, other online gaming services also became available. They were similar, and used by the Sony PlayStation and other consoles.

Xbox Live has made a huge difference in gaming. Because of it, Bryan has competed against many new people. He has even competed against players in countries as far away as Australia. Day or night, there are thousands of people all over the world playing *Halo*. Sometimes they play by themselves in single-player "campaign" mode. They try to complete the different levels that are part of *Halo*'s plot. Most gamers use the multiplayer mode, though. This connects them with other online players.

One big part of online gaming is communication. Wearing headsets, people are able to talk strategy with their teammates. That's not all—there's plenty of "trash talking" going on between opponents. This annoys some people, but it can add to the competition and the fun. Even pros do this sometimes. It's a way of playing mind games with their opponents.

Bryan couldn't wait for the release of *Halo 2*. The very first time he played it, he was hooked. "I knew right away how awesome it was," Bryan says. "I didn't want to do anything else but play *Halo 2* for a long time."

He wasn't alone. People all across the country were buying *Halo 2*. The reasons were obvious: amazing graphics, worldwide competition, and playing on teams with friends. Every day, gamers would meet their friends online, form a team, and play. Bryan's career is a perfect example of how online gaming connects people. His MLG teammates don't even live in Florida. They are spread out all over the country. Yet it's the same as if they lived next door.

In making the switch to *Halo 2*, Bryan had big goals. "I wanted to be number one on the 'leader board' legitimately," he explains. "At that time there was a lot of cheating going on. That's actually how I got my nickname."

Bryan Rizzo, or "Legit," tells the whole story. It happened about a month after *Halo 2* came out. His friend "TuSick" asked Bryan to join his *Halo 2* team. At the time, Bryan was frustrated by the dishonesty of some players. There was a trick known as "standbying." The host player could freeze out other players and win games easily. This boosted the host's ranking. It was cheating, and it messed up the ranking system. That's important, because the ranking system is a big part of *Halo 2*.

Bryan didn't want to boost his own ranking in that way. Besides, what was the point? Eventually, these posers would be uncovered in tournaments—if they even had the guts to show up. "That's not my style," he told his friend. "I always keep it *legit*."

Pressure: Legit and his teammates in a tight match.

With that statement, "Legit" was born. Back then he wasn't famous or anything. He was just a ninth grader who loved *Halo 2*. Before long, Legit would become a gaming superstar.

Chapter Three

Competitor

It was November of 2005, a year after *Halo 2* had been released. 15-year-old Bryan was looking forward to a weekend trip to Huntsville, Alabama. Bryan's mother is from Alabama, so this was a chance for them to visit family. Bryan has always had a good time hanging out there. He spends time with his grandparents, as well as his cousins and Uncle William.

Luckily for Bryan, Uncle William had found out something interesting. A *Halo 2* tournament was taking place the same weekend as Bryan's visit. Uncle William remembered that his nephew always talked about *Halo*. Without hesitation, he picked up the phone. He asked Bryan if he should sign him up for the tournament. The entry fee was only $5.

A Saturn rocket prepares for lift-off a few miles from the home of Bryan's grandmother, at the U.S. Space & Rocket Center in Huntsville, Alabama.

When Bryan arrived in Huntsville, he was happy to see all of his relatives. But his mind was wandering. After all, it was already Friday night. In less than 12 hours, the tournament would begin. Bryan had played a lot of *Halo* in his life. In his heart he felt that he was a very good player. Still, he wasn't totally sure. The tournament would be a chance for him to measure himself against other good players.

The next morning, Bryan and his family drove over to the large hall in Huntsville. It was crowded and noisy inside. Without much experience playing tournaments, Bryan was nervous. His heart started racing and his palms were sweaty.

The tournament was an individual event. This was lucky because Bryan wasn't part of any team in Alabama. The format was simple: Everyone who had signed up would be competing against each other. Many skilled players were there, because prize money was being offered.

The rules said that there would be three rounds. Those who scored high enough in round one would advance to round two. That would be the semifinal. In that round, all but eight players would be eliminated. Those top eight players would then square off in round three—the finals.

To Bryan's surprise, he was the top player in the first round. Nobody was even within 40 kills of him! People started talking about this stranger from Florida, who was destroying the entire field. Everybody wondered if Legit was the real deal. The true test would come in the next round. That's when the competition would get tougher.

During the lunch break, Bryan felt confident. Of course, he knew that he was a target now. As the guy in first place, everybody would be gunning for him. He would have to respond. For months he had been playing online from his home. Now, he was in a huge room, in front of a large television set. All eyes were on him.

The second round was exciting, especially when a skilled opponent stepped up. He was a teenager known as "Bama Country Boy." He shot to the top of the field, leaving Bryan stuck in second place. "Bama" was good—even Bryan had to admit it. On top of that, he was the local hero. It seemed that he had brought everyone he knew to the tournament. The crowd was going wild, yelling and screaming with every kill Bama made.

The pressure of playing in front of a live audience can often weigh down an inexperienced player.

Later on, the main event got underway. It was the finals, which meant that it was put-up or shut-up time. Most of the attention was being given to Legit and Bama. They were clearly the favorites. Legit and Bama looked at each other but didn't speak. They were ready to let their skills do the talking.

The action was insane. Legit and Bama held their controllers tightly while their fingers whipped around. The fans were really into it at this point. They were definitely on Bama's side, cheering loudly for him.

As soon as the finals began, a change took place in Bryan. Sure, Bama was a great player. He was also three years older than Bryan. It didn't matter, though. Bryan was in a zone. He didn't care about the fans sitting behind him, or the giant television sets. Legit was doing battle in the world of *Halo*. In this world, he was James Bond, Indiana Jones, and the Terminator all mixed in one. He was unstoppable.

When it was all over, Bryan had won by almost 30 kills. It was now official: He *was* different—he had a gift. Sure, this was just a small local tournament. Still, it marked the beginning of a new chapter in the life of Bryan Rizzo. He had entered an unknown competition and dealt with the pressure.

As if Bryan wasn't stoked already, things were about to get even better. He was called up for the trophy presentation. Photographers were taking pictures. Bryan was nervous and excited, but it was a feeling that he will always remember. "I'm a pretty normal and humble guy," he says. "But at that moment, I felt like a celebrity!"

As the awards ceremony ended, Bryan was given the winner's check for $1,000. He couldn't believe it. He had entered a tournament that had a $5 entry fee, and walked away with $1,000!

The next day, Bryan returned to Florida and went back to school. He proudly showed his friends the check. They were blown away. Seeing the check in Bryan's hand, they realized something. Gaming could become more than just a hobby. Bryan realized the same thing. He wondered: *Am I good enough to go pro?*

It was time to take the next step and find out. Bryan could have joined any gaming league, but he chose MLG. They have big-time sponsors and huge prize money. MLG is an important organization in the gaming business. This is an industry that brings in several billion dollars a year. Talk about being "legit"—interactive entertainment is *barely* behind movies and music in terms of earning money.

Bryan knew that becoming an MLG pro wouldn't be easy. Rising up in MLG takes hard work and dedication, as well as talent. MLG is a professional league, just like other sports leagues. Players travel to different cities, which host tournaments as part of the MLG season. Great rewards are in store for the top players: prize money, fame, sponsorship, and even pro contracts.

Unlike youth sports, professional video game tournaments don't go by age. Bryan was just as likely to go up against someone in his 20s as someone his own age. This is similar to the X Games, which includes teenagers like Ryan Sheckler. Ryan is a pro skateboarder. That means he has to compete against adults such as Paul Rodriguez, Jr. and Bucky Lasek.

Whether someone is young or old, it's not easy to get to a professional level. MLG has three divisions: pro, semi-pro, and amateur. The pros are the players ranked in the top 16. Then come the semi-pros, who are the players ranked from 17 to 32. All other players are considered amateurs. Luckily, MLG gives amateurs the chance to prove themselves. They do this with "open-registration" tournaments.

These open-registration events are very important, especially for those who do well. The best amateurs are invited to compete with the pros. That's a great opportunity for an amateur.

Bryan wanted to play both as an individual *and* as part of a team. The individual events are known as "FFA," which stands for "Free-For-All." These events are similar to the tournament that he played in Alabama.

The first step was finding a good team to play with. That was going to be hard. The top pro teams would never take a chance on an unknown guy. Bryan quickly learned the best way to become a pro: He had to sign up and go to the tournaments. He needed to make a name for himself in FFA, as an individual. He also needed to play on amateur teams. If he performed well, people would take notice. His hope was to draw the attention of a top pro team.

It's always tough trying to establish yourself in a new situation, especially one as competitive as MLG.

Bryan started focusing on specific gametypes. This would boost his chances of becoming a pro. There are many ways to play *Halo 2*—in other words, many different "gametypes." To make things fair, only certain gametypes are played at MLG tournaments. Players visit www.mlgpro.com and click on the events page. That shows them exactly which gametypes will be used at each tournament. Bryan wanted to improve his skills in those gametypes.

Another thing Bryan learned was to focus on *how* he was playing video games. It wasn't just about fun anymore. To compete with top players, he had to continue improving. He played hour after hour, thinking about game strategy. He was hard on himself, but only because he wanted to reach a higher level. He worked on the weak parts of his game.

Gamers know that everyone has strengths and weaknesses. A great *Halo 2* team is one in which players work well with each other. It doesn't help if each player is skilled at the same thing. On a top team, everybody has to be good at some specific part of the game.

A team also has to fit together well as a group. Sometimes that means taking charge as a leader, or controlling certain weapons. Other times it means understanding maps, or simply supporting your team-mates. If players want to be famous all by themselves, they should only play in FFA. Teams that work well together usually have the most success.

Bryan was excited about his thrilling victory in Alabama. Still, he knew he had his work cut out for him. It helps that MLG wipes the slate clean at the beginning of every season. This gives a new player the chance to make a name for himself. And that was exactly what 15-year-old Bryan planned on doing.

Legit gets his MLG career underway.

Chapter Four

Pro

Bryan's pro career got off to a fast start in late 2005. It was just after the tournament in Alabama. In his very first MLG event, he finished in the top 16 in the FFA category. This gave him a boost of confidence. It also started turning some heads in the gaming world. In his second tournament, Bryan finished in the top 10. He was making good progress. Next, it was on to Chicago for Bryan's third MLG tournament. He was hoping to continue his success there.

Bryan caught fire at the Chicago event. He did well as an individual, but even better in the team game. His amateur team came in first place! Because of it, they were moved up to the pro division. Bryan and his teammates did very well there, finishing in the top eight of the pro division.

When Bryan looks back on his performance in Chicago, he says, "Having the chance to play with the pros was my big break. That's what an amateur wants—a shot at the best players in the world. It was a great experience." Bryan gained a lot more than experience, though. A lot of pro teams saw how good he was. They started keeping an eye on him.

Professional video game teams sometimes break up or lose a player. When this happens, they need to find someone new. This situation occurs in the music world as well. A band will sometimes have to replace a drummer or singer. So they are always on the lookout for talented people. It's the same way with gaming. That's why MLG pros always notice up-and-coming gamers.

When it comes to the team game, nobody has been more successful than "Final Boss." Bryan hoped to join a team that could challenge their dynasty.

In Chicago, Legit proved that he was a rising star. Still, he wasn't satisfied. He knew he had to continue improving. He wanted to hang with the top players all the time, not just at one tournament.

Chicago, a beautiful and vibrant city ... and the scene of many of Legit's greatest successes.

"Any talented player can be good as an individual," Bryan explains. "This is especially true if they have good shots and skills. But getting used to the team game is a different story. You have to learn how to deal with tough situations. Also, you have to learn how to outsmart other players. It becomes as much about your head as it is about your fingers."

As a pro, Bryan has learned many new things. For example, there are times when he has to be patient and *not* make any kills. Why? Maybe he's protecting a teammate who has a more important weapon. If Bryan can help his teammate stay safe, that could help his team win.

Bryan explains this point by talking about baseball. He says that sometimes a guy is brought into the game to bunt. In that situation, there is already a runner on base. The idea is to make an out. Still, a good bunt will advance the runner to the next base. However, when a player bunts, he gives up the chance to hit a home run. He does it for the benefit of the team. Bryan puts it this way: "That guy never gets the headlines. But sometimes that bunt is the difference between winning and losing."

This is a pretty complicated way to look at video games. But that's what makes pros like Bryan so good. They always seem to be one step ahead of the competition. Their moves within the game are smooth and fast. Pros make their way through dangerous situations with ease. They don't stop and wonder which button to press, or which way to go. Pros travel through cyber worlds with confidence. They know exactly what to expect around the next corner.

Like all sports, there are huge differences between amateurs and pros. Many gamers mention hand-eye coordination. Others talk about talent, and understanding the game itself. Bryan feels that there is something even beyond skill and practice: concentration. Among the top players, the smallest advantage can mean the difference between winning and losing. That's why pro cyber athletes stay focused at all times.

Gamers concentrate at a crucial moment. The audience looks on anxiously.

With his improved skills, Bryan was soon picked up by an outstanding team. This was no surprise. After all, his reputation in MLG was growing. He had barely missed qualifying for the 2005 National Championships . . . as a rookie. He was like a Minor League pitcher with a great arm. For a pitcher like that, it's just a matter of time until he reaches the Major Leagues. In Bryan's case, he was ready for the Major Leagues of gaming—MLG.

It happened in the off-season, before the start of the 2006 season. Bryan received a phone call from members of "Storm Ventures." This was a big deal.

Storm Ventures was a pro team in MLG. Any amateur would have been thrilled to be on their team. So they could have chosen anyone they wanted.

"At first, they just wanted to try it out," Bryan remembers. "So we made plans to meet online and play against one of the best teams. I guess that was their way of testing me. They wanted to see if I could handle the pressure of tough opponents." Bryan was up for the challenge. That night, he helped Storm Ventures win the majority of the games.

That was all Storm Ventures needed to see. They invited Legit to join their team for the upcoming 2006 season. Bryan was stoked, and he said yes right away. He went into training, along with his new teammates. Their names were "Ramby," "Naded," and "Pwn."

Storm Ventures.

Storm Ventures started practicing together soon after that. They focused on the *Halo 2* gametypes that would be played during the 2006 MLG season. Some of these games might sound familiar. One of them is called "Capture the Flag." The goal is to steal your opponent's flag and return it to your home base. The first team to capture it five times is the winner.

Another game is "Oddball," which is like "Keep Away." Both teams try to hang on to the skull-shaped oddball for five minutes. Sometimes neither team can do this by the end of the game. In that case, it comes down to the number of minutes each team has hung on to it. The results are added up. The team with the most time is the winner.

The third and final game was Bryan's favorite: "Team Slayer" is all about the kills. Nothing else matters. First team to 50 wins, plain and simple.

MLG tournaments are all double-elimination. This means that when a team loses one game, they aren't finished yet. They are placed in the "loser's bracket." If they lose again, they are automatically eliminated. In the loser's bracket, the goal is to win all of the games. Any team that does this is put back in the main field. Then they still have a chance to win the tournament.

As everyone knows, a tournament can only have one winner. For teams that don't win, though, every game still counts. That's because points are awarded for each game won. At the end of the season, the points are all added up. This decides who makes the playoffs. In 2006, only the top eight teams would make it. They would receive an invitation to Las Vegas for the National Championships.

All roads lead to Vegas, as Bryan and his new team look ahead to the 2006 season.

Bryan had a lot of motivation to work hard for the upcoming 2006 season. That's why he spent many hours online practicing with his teammates. He also found other ways to improve. He started training for his sport with the same determination that pro athletes in other sports display.

Bryan's routine became pretty consistent. He started going to the gym several times a week. This is something that he still does. He's always been in good shape, going back to his days as a baseball player. Now, the stakes have become higher. Most people don't realize that some gamers think about being strong and in good condition. Actually, it can be a key part of a successful game plan. Simply put, if a cyber athlete is in good shape, he or she can play better.

Many gamers play for several hours in a row. It can be very tiring. When this happens, your mind can wander. A strong body and a strong mind make a huge difference.

Bryan also does hand and wrist exercises. There's an injury that sometimes happens to people who type on computers all day. It's called "carpal tunnel syndrome." Their wrists can become very sore. It can get so bad that they are unable to do their work. For a gamer, this would make it impossible to play. Bryan doesn't want this to happen to him. So he does exercises to stay loose and flexible. His favorite one is to rotate his wrists forward and backward, up and down.

Not only does Legit take care of his body, but he also takes care of his mind. He works hard in school because he knows that a good education will help him achieve his future goals. He has seen the gaming industry from the inside and knows how much competition there is for jobs. With his 3.2 grade point average, Bryan has a lot of confidence. He feels that a career in the interactive entertainment industry is definitely in his future. Who knows, maybe someday he'll help create *Halo 6*!

Chapter Five

The World of Halo

Halo is one of the most successful video games of all time. Of course, there never would have been *Halo* if video games had never been invented. Bryan knows a lot about the history of video games. Most people don't realize that the video game business started over 50 years ago. That was *way* before Xbox, PlayStation, or any of the other modern gaming systems.

Progress happened slowly over time. This is typical of many important inventions, in almost all fields. For example, Henry Ford originally dreamed up the automobile in the late 1800s. Yet it wasn't until 1908 that his famous Model T was first introduced to people. Cars have certainly come a long way since then. Imagine if Mr. Ford could see modern cars, with DVD players and navigation systems.

The modern age of video games began in the 1970s. The first gaming console in American homes was called the Magnavox Odyssey. The Odyssey wasn't very successful at first. Then things began to change. Along came *Pong*, Atari's popular arcade game. *Pong* was soon followed by famous games like *Space Invaders*, *Donkey Kong*, and *Pac-Man*. These early games were simple, but very popular. As time went on, companies kept putting out new games and consoles.

The Magnavox Odyssey: It may be hard to believe, but in 1972 this was considered a very high-tech gaming device.

By the mid-1980s, Nintendo was the leader in the video game business. Its gaming console was sold with a popular new game called *Super Mario Bros.*

Young people jumped at it. Years later, Nintendo also released a hand-held console. It was called the Game Boy and it became famous.

The original Nintendo Entertainment System.

As the 1990s rolled around, advances were coming at a very fast pace. Sega Genesis was invented, followed by the first PlayStation. Things were really starting to get exciting. That's why it was no surprise when Microsoft decided to get into the mix. Microsoft is one of the most valuable companies on Earth. The company is worth approximately $300 billion.

Microsoft noticed that the gaming business was booming. They wanted to get involved, so they started working on a new video game console. It would come to be known as Xbox. Of course, there were already many well-known gaming consoles on the market. Microsoft needed something special to capture the attention of gamers. They wanted a fantastic game—one that was so amazing, it would make people buy the Xbox.

This is the Washington State headquarters of Microsoft, a company that employs more than 50,000 people worldwide.

Enter *Halo: Combat Evolved*, otherwise known as *Halo*. It was created by a company called Bungie Studios. They had also created many other great games. *Halo* was different, though. With its incredible graphics and exciting story, it was awesome. The people at Bungie had been working on it for many years. Their hard work paid off when Microsoft decided to buy Bungie Studios. They actually bought the entire company! Microsoft had a good reason for doing this, of course—they were bringing *Halo* exclusively to the Xbox.

On November 15, 2001, *Halo* was released. Video game experts were amazed. They said that *Halo* was one of the greatest video games ever created. *Halo* was a huge hit right away. Everybody wanted to buy an Xbox and play—either alone or with friends. Sometimes people had their friends come over and set up their Xbox consoles. In this way, they could all play together. This was actually the beginning of multiplayer. Later on, it would get even better with the arrival of Xbox Live and *Halo 2*.

For the time being, *Halo* was just fine for everybody. It was awesome. The idea behind *Halo* is really cool. The game focuses on a war between humans and alien races. The alien races are known as the Covenant. In the game, humans live on many different planets. These different planets are where many of the battles take place.

Unfortunately, over time the Covenant is slowly winning the war. Its goal is to wipe out the human race. It looks for humans anywhere it can find them. It *really* wants to discover the location of Earth. Luckily, the good guys have the "Master Chief." He's a powerful soldier, and one of the main characters. He wants to stop the Covenant from reaching its goal.

Halo is a fantastic, first-person shooting game with a ton of action. The original was great, but all it did was make fans want more. Before long, everybody was waiting for *Halo 2* to come out. When it finally did, it offered a lot of advances. There were new weapons, vehicles, maps, and a smarter computer opponent. But the main improvement was the Xbox Live online service.

Halo fans like Bryan were now able to compete with people online. Going "live" changed everything. It's one of the reasons that the *Halo* series continues to be popular. Actually, it has become one of the best-selling video game series of all time. *Halo 3* was released in the fall of 2007, adding to the interest.

Think about how many people are buying and playing video games these days. Xboxes and PlayStations are now as common in American homes as microwaves and dishwashers. Sales of computer and video games add up to more than $7 billion a year in the United States. That means that video games are catching up to music and movies. Two out of every three households have at least one family member who is playing video games. So what's the bottom line? Gaming is getting bigger and bigger, with no end in sight. There are many reasons for this. The most obvious one is the fact that games have become much more advanced and fun to play. Gamers are quick to point to the graphics and the gameplay itself.

Tournaments have also made gaming more popular. There are major tournaments out there for many popular video games. One of them is for *Madden NFL 07*, which was the top-selling video game in 2006. It sold an amazing total of 1.6 million copies—and that was just for PlayStation!

Just like the tournaments that Bryan plays in, *Madden* tournaments are huge. Check out what happened to 16-year-old Ayan Tariq: Ayan, whose video game name is "Fool," traveled to Hawaii for the 2006 EA Sports Madden Challenge. He ended up winning it . . . and he earned $100,000!

It's not only pro gamers like Fool who enjoy *Madden* tournaments—even NFL stars want to play. Every year, during Super Bowl weekend, the "Madden

Bowl" is held. This event is just for fun and bragging rights. Some of football's biggest stars compete against each other in the video game tournament. Everyone has a blast, including the people watching. This friendly competition is even shown on ESPN.

There's another reason why video games are more popular these days: the controllers. They have continued to improve. They now respond much better to the movements of a gamer's fingers.

Pictured above is a modern PlayStation contoller.

In the early years, controllers had uncomfortable shapes and keypads with numbers. Also, the buttons were placed in awkward positions. Over time, more modern controllers were invented. They had curved handles and sensitive joysticks, and were easier to use.

Modern controllers let you move three-dimensionally and in all different directions. This technology makes games more realistic, and it also makes movements more precise. It's totally different from the controllers that were made in the old days. With old controllers, you could only move forward, back, up, and down. It's more fun when movements in cyberspace are like movements in the real world.

Primitive by comparison: Pictured above is an Atari controller from the 1980s (not exactly high-tech).

The modern Xbox controller is similar to the one made by Sony for the PlayStation. These two big companies are competitors, of course. There's also a cool new controller that may change gameplay forever. Made by Nintendo for the Wii, it adds a more physical element to gameplay.

The Wii, which arrived in late 2006, became popular right away. It has a controller that responds to arm and body motion. It also responds to normal finger movements. Anyone who has played on the Wii would agree that it's a lot of fun to actually feel like you're throwing a football, or casting out your fishing line. Players are almost *in* the action.

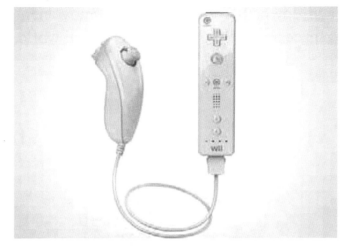

The Nintendo Wii controller.

The Wii will force other companies to make their own games and consoles even better. That's what the video game business is all about. Progress is important, and it's one of the main reasons that gamers are so loyal. That's why millions of games have been sold in the United States. Even back in 2004, people bought over 250 million computer and video games. That's an average of almost two games for every single home in America.

Pretty amazing for such a new form of entertainment. After all, video games have only been popular for the last 20 years or so. They are still on the rise. Who can even *imagine* where things will be in five or 10 years?

Chapter Six

Life on the Road

As the 2006 MLG season began, the members of Storm Ventures felt confident. Legit, Ramby, Naded, and Pwn had been practicing every day. Bryan always talks about the importance of team chemistry. He knew that Storm Ventures had a lot of it.

In a team game, strategy is also very important. "We spent a lot of time talking about strategy," Bryan remembers. "We went through every map and figured out what we wanted to do. We discussed different ways to take control of the map." All of their hard work started to pay off. By the middle of the season, Storm Ventures was one of the top teams in MLG.

Besides the team game, Bryan did very well as an individual. Still, nothing mattered more to him than being a part of a good team. It was especially fun because he and the guys were winning. As they traveled to each new tournament, Storm Ventures had a great time. They were getting paid just to hang out and play *Halo*! In addition to the money he earned, Bryan received other cool stuff—like a free cell phone from Boost Mobile.

After nearly two years of competing, Bryan still gets hyped when he goes to an MLG event. Tournaments take place between Friday and Sunday. Pros like Bryan don't actually compete until Saturday, though. Friday is always a travel day. Bryan's parents usually go with him, although he travels alone once in a while. When he and his parents land, they go straight from the airport to the hotel, where the tournament takes place.

After getting to the hotel, Bryan signs in at the tournament. The rest of Friday evening is spent practicing. He also hangs out with his teammates, which is always the best part. They spend so much time on the Internet together, so it's nice to actually see one another in person.

Chillin' at the hotel.

The first night is pretty crazy. Bryan's older teammates usually have their own rooms, so they all hang out there. They also run around the hotel for some friendly trash talk with the other pros. In the world of MLG, everyone knows each other. Yes, they are all opponents, but many of them are also good friends. Either way, when the games begin, it's all about winning.

The first event takes place on Friday night, but it's for amateurs only. This is the open FFA (Free-For-All). That's how amateurs make a name for themselves. Remember, Bryan first started his MLG career in that way. A victory in the open FFA earns amateur competitors a shot at pros like Bryan. That takes place the following night, in the championship FFA.

Saturday is the beginning of the main event—the tournament for pro teams. It's called the championship 4v4. Meanwhile, the open FFA tournament continues for the amateurs. This all happens during the day, and then there is a dinner break. Things really start to heat up on Saturday night, after dinner. The early rounds of 4v4 continue. Then, usually between 9 p.m. and midnight, the championship FFA is played.

Sunday is just as intense. The later rounds of the championship 4v4 are played. That takes most of the day. By the early evening, it's time for one last game: the championship. This is the end of a long and exciting weekend.

Bryan was on the MLG pro circuit for the whole year in 2006. It was the most fun he ever had in his life. He traveled from city to city. The circuit started out in New Jersey, followed by trips to Texas, California, and Illinois. Another stop was in Orlando, Florida, which is only 100 miles from Bryan's home. His family and friends came to Orlando to watch him compete in person. As the season ended, the playoffs were held in

New York. Finally, the National Championships took place in Las Vegas.

2006 was an important year for Major League Gaming. It was exciting because there was a reality series on TV about MLG. The show was on the USA Network. This gave the entire country a chance to see amazing gamers like Legit.

Denise Rizzo, Bryan's mother, was very impressed. She says, "Seeing Bryan on TV was wonderful. It showed how popular this whole thing has become. It's easy to see why it's so important to Bryan."

By the time the 2006 season ended, Legit had accomplished a great deal. He was now considered a top FFA player. Remember, Bryan had only played a few events in 2005. This was almost like his rookie season. Yet he finished in the top eight in *every* MLG tournament held in 2006. He also scored huge wins over some of the best players in the world.

In the team competition, Storm Ventures enjoyed their best year ever. The highlight of their season happened in Chicago. That's the city where Bryan had played as an amateur just one year earlier. In fact, that's where he had been noticed by Storm Ventures for the first time.

Now, one year later, he was a big part of Storm Ventures. He and his teammates caught fire. They made it all the way to the championship match. The league champions, Final Boss, were waiting for them. The match was hard-fought and went down to the wire. Even though Storm Ventures ended up losing, they earned a lot of respect.

After their success in Chicago, Storm Ventures was on a roll. They continued doing well, and made it to the National Championships in Las Vegas. When the season was complete, they had finished in the top seven overall.

The members of Storm Ventures were very happy. It felt great to know that they could deal with the pressure. Bryan certainly doesn't run away from pressure. As a matter of fact, he loves it. He doesn't care if it's a small tournament like the one in Alabama—or an event that is shown on national TV. He has always been able to handle the tough situations. "I like taking on challenges," he says. "Some people press a little bit or overplay. I just try to stay steady and focus on what needs to be done."

In one year, Bryan had gone from an unknown amateur to a solid MLG pro. His individual ranking had zoomed all the way to number *three*. The 2006 season came to an end with Legit as one of the top cyber athletes in America.

Chapter Seven

A College Degree ... in Video Games?

The alarm clock woke Bryan up very early. It was a Wednesday morning in 2006 during spring break. He would have liked to stay in bed for another few hours, but he couldn't. Bryan's family had planned a trip that he wasn't looking forward to: Bryan was going to college.

No, he wasn't going to college to study. He was still only a sophomore in high school. His brother Tyler, on the other hand, was a senior. Tyler was interested in a college named the University of Central Florida. Most people call it UCF for short. It's located about 100 miles from the Rizzos' home in Palm Harbor.

Tyler was thinking about the field of hospitality as a possible career choice. Hospitality means providing service to people in places like hotels and restaurants. His top choice was theme park management, which is a category of hospitality. This career teaches people how to manage places like Disney World or Six Flags. Tyler had always loved theme parks, so why not be around them for his whole life? The Rizzos were checking out UCF because the school has an excellent hospitality program.

Ever since they were very young, both Tyler and Bryan have loved amusement parks.

What did all of this have to do with Bryan? Well, like Tyler, he has also made a decision about his future: He loves the world of video games and always wants to be around them. Bryan will be a pro gamer for as long as possible, of course. But he knows that he will not be able to do it forever. Even famous athletes have to retire at some point. That day will come for Bryan eventually. Luckily, it won't be the end of the road for his video game career.

There are thousands of young people who share Bryan's love for gaming. There's something many of them may not know. If they get a great education, they can be around video games forever! That's because there are many careers in the video game business.

In America, the video game business provides 5,000 new jobs every year. These jobs are in fields such as game design, art, computer programming, and testing. Are you interested in interactive entertainment? If so, you should know more about your career opportunities.

These opportunities exist because of the games themselves. How is a video game created? The same way a book, a song, or a movie begins: with an idea. It might be an idea from something that's already in our world. An example of that is *John Madden Football*. Or it could be something brand new, like the world of *Halo*.

Coming up with an idea for a game is only the first step. There are many people who are involved in creating a video game. Big games like *Halo* have hundreds of people in the mix. Some of them are called producers. They're involved with everything. They make decisions, meet with people, and figure out how much money to spend. Producers get involved from the very first day. It can take years until the game is finished and ready to be sold.

A programmer is another important person involved in the creation of a video game. Programmers create the computer code that makes the game actually work. It's a difficult job because programming is a different language. Learning it takes years of education and training. It's not easy, but programmers get to be involved in exciting new projects. They can also earn a lot of money.

To some people it may look like jibberish, but program code brings exciting video games to life.

Next up is the artist, whose job is to make everything look great. There are many young people who are talented in drawing, painting, and computer graphics. They are in luck because good artists are always needed at software companies. Thousands of artists work at companies such as Sony, Microsoft, and Nintendo.

Digital art: An artist uses a graphics tablet to create video game images.

There is a good reason for this. All someone has to do is look at the amazing graphics in games like *Halo* or *Half-Life*. How about sports games like *NBA Live*? LeBron James and Kobe Bryant didn't just jump into the game. It takes a lot of skilled people to make all these NBA superstars look and act so real. Attention is paid to every detail. They even make the shooting and dribbling style look like the player's.

Writers can get great jobs in video games as well. In the old days, the programmers and artists would make up the stories. Now, writers are hired to develop the story ideas. This might be why modern games like *Halo* have such original and complex story lines.

Some people are not interested in programming, art, or writing. That's okay—these people can still have careers in the video game business. There are hundreds of other good jobs, such as advertising. Sure, it takes creative people to invent a game. But the people who work on the business side are *just* as important.

Think about it. What if a company creates the most incredible game but nobody ever hears about it? Well, that game will not sell. Have you ever had the experience of liking a band that isn't well known? The natural thing to do is talk to your friends about it. You'll probably also play your favorite songs for them. When you do this, you are "advertising" something.

It's pretty much the same way in the video game world of advertising and promotion. A perfect example is Bungie Studios. They did their job by creating *Halo*, one of the most awesome games ever. Microsoft spent a lot of money to advertise it. They made television commercials and took out magazines ads. Because of that, millions of people heard about *Halo*. That's a good thing. Otherwise, *Halo* could have ended up as a fantastic—but unknown—game.

Bryan has thought about many careers in the video game business. The one he likes the most at this point is event planning. This career means exactly what it says: planning video game events. Bryan knows what it takes to do a job like this. He sees it at every tournament he goes to.

It takes a lot of skill to host a video game tournament. A lot of people show up, so you have to be organized. You have to plan meals, equipment, and hotel rooms for the players. That's only the beginning. Someone has to be in charge of every single detail. In the future, Bryan wants to be that person.

Event planning is an interesting profession, epecially when it's on a large scale ... like MLG tournaments.

The purpose of the Rizzos' trip to college that morning was for Tyler to check out UCF. Bryan thought he was just going along to be with his family. On the drive over, however, he learned something that shocked him. The University of Central Florida offers a degree in video games! Talk about a perfect fit. The actual name of the degree is Interactive Entertainment. As we've learned, that's a general term for the entire video game industry.

For Bryan, the day was long, but interesting. He found out that these types of degrees are now offered at most colleges across the country. He also saw what life is like for students at UCF. There's so much to learn about the video game business. The program at UCF teaches it all with lots of hands-on training. Students even get to form teams and create real video games. That's a homework assignment Bryan would definitely enjoy.

When it comes to relaxing and taking a break from work, students at UCF have it made. They can kick back in the huge lounge. It's complete with a 60-inch, flat-screen TV, PlayStation 3, *and* Xbox 360. Bryan could definitely see himself spending his free time hanging out there.

College students interested in Interactive Entertainment learn wide-ranging skills. For Bryan, who is leaning toward event planning, understanding how to deal with the media is important. Luckily, as an MLG star, he has plenty of experience in this area. He's shown here being interviewed at a tournament.

When the day was over, Bryan had a lot to think about. He'll have plenty of decisions to make in the future, including which college to attend. "There's one thing I've learned from all my experiences," Bryan says. "Life has a ton of opportunities. After college, I may end up working for a company that creates video games. Or maybe I'll do event planning for MLG. It all sounds good to me."

Chapter Eight

Gamer for Life

Video games have been very good to Bryan Rizzo. Because of them, he's had incredible experiences and made lifelong friends. He's even learned about possible career choices. That's not all. As a gamer who plays in pro tournaments, Bryan has earned a lot of money.

Bryan also earns money by giving online lessons on how to improve in *Halo 2*. As part of their lessons, students even get to compete on practice teams with him. Bryan likes helping people, so he does it whenever he can. People really enjoy learning from someone as skilled as Legit. They contact him through MLG or through his MySpace page.

Playing under the name "Perfect Storm" in a non-MLG event, Bryan and his teammates find themselves in the usual spot: the winner's circle.

Bryan has a jam-packed schedule and always seems to be busy. Still, he loves the life of a cyber athlete. He feels that video games have gotten a bum rap by most adults. Many of them didn't even grow up playing them. So they don't quite understand why video games are so much fun. They also don't realize that playing video games can actually be *good* for people.

It's been proven that video games can make your reflexes sharper. They can also improve hand-eye coordination, and even help make learning easier. Many surgeons have to perform life-and-death operations. Some of them play video games as a way to keep their fingers loose. Video games that re-create emergency conditions can also play an important role in training paramedics and firefighters.

The police and the military have used video game technology as well. Games have been created for soldiers. It lets them see what it's like to be on a battlefield. They can also learn how to make split-second decisions. Pilots use flight-simulator programs to practice landing planes in dangerous situations. This technology can make air travel safer.

The flight simulator pictured above is the ultimate virtual reality flying experience.

Even the world of sports has caught on. This isn't surprising when you consider how many amazing sports video games there are. Several baseball teams have bought pitching machines that use video game technology. Some football coaches and players have also experimented with video games. It makes sense that playing *John Madden Football* may help a player prepare for a big game.

Almost everybody can agree that video games are enjoyable and even good for our world. There are many examples of this. Being social and meeting people with similar interests is one of them. Bryan has met a lot of friends through online gaming.

Another person who loves video games as much as Bryan is Brice Mellen. You might even say that they changed his life. Brice, who started playing video games at the age of seven, is now in college. He's a whiz at *Mortal Kombat* and *Soul Caliber*. His dream is to go into video game programming. It won't be a surprise if he makes it. Brice is the kind of person who never lets anything stand in his way. That's saying a lot, because Brice has been blind since the day he was born.

That's right, a skilled gamer who can't even see the screen. Talk about determination! The first question everybody asks is obvious: *How does he play?* Well, Brice is able to remember moves and joystick operations. When he first gets a game, he asks a lot of questions. Then, by listening carefully to sounds in the game, he is able to play—and play well. Brice's "never-quit" attitude is a true inspiration.

Bryan agrees. He has worked very hard also. You don't become a pro gamer by accident. Like Brice, video games have played a major role in Bryan's life. They have changed him in many ways. Bryan says that video games are an outstanding activity that all kids can enjoy. However, he's seen some of the dangers as well.

Bryan doesn't make a big deal about it. He simply says that video games should fit into a person's life—but not be the *only* thing. "I've seen some insane things," Bryan says. "I've seen kids get addicted to video games. They get so into it that nothing else matters to them. It's messed up. I think they just spend so much time playing games that they forget about their lives outside of them."

He's right. It's sad to see articles in the newspaper about young people like that. They just sit around all day in front of their computer, Xbox, or PlayStation. Yes, there's a lot of proof about how positive and productive video games can be. Unfortunately, there is also another side. There is proof that kids who don't exercise are at risk for serious health problems.

One of those problems is a disease called diabetes. It occurs when the human body has trouble keeping its blood sugar at the proper level. Diabetes can lead to all kinds of medical problems such as heart disease and blindness. As many as 200,000 *kids* in the United States may have type 1 diabetes. The problem has gotten worse. Some experts wonder if the technological revolution is partly to blame. They point to the rise in childhood obesity and cases of type 1 diabetes.

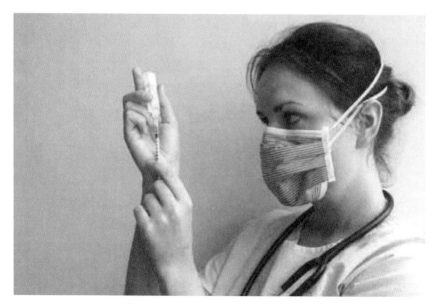

A doctor prepares to give a diabetic patient a shot.

Video games alone can't be blamed for these conditions, of course. Balance is the key to any happy life. Even a pro like Legit understands this. He strikes a balance between the hours he spends in cyberspace and the real world. He has a bunch of friends who aren't gamers. He still likes to have fun and hang out with them.

Bryan is also careful never to put video games above his schoolwork. His 3.2 grade point average is proof of that. Nobody loves video games more than he does. Still, it's not going to stop him from being healthy and feeling great.

Taking a break from video games, Bryan enjoys a beautiful Florida day.

Legit's gaming career continues to progress. Each new MLG season lets him test his skills against the best players in the world. More importantly, he continues to learn and improve. He is moving further down the path he has chosen. Bryan has big plans for his future, and nobody doubts that his dreams will all come true. It's pretty hard to doubt a guy who has accomplished so much. When Bryan Rizzo sets his mind to something, he usually succeeds.

Bryan's hard work has led to great rewards ... just check out his license plate below.

For now, Bryan is looking forward to enjoying every last minute of high school. In a couple of years, he'll head off to college. That will be the beginning of a new challenge for him. Whether he ends up at UCF or somewhere else, he is sure of one thing: "No matter where I go or what I do, I'm a gamer for life."

The world continues to change at a fast pace. Who can imagine what things will look like 10 or 20 years down the road? What will be the next great advance in technology? Who will design the games and create the Web sites? Who will dream up the newest advances in interactive entertainment? Very possibly, it will be teenagers like Bryan Rizzo . . . or the young people reading this book. These future stars will take our world in exciting and new directions.

Video games are just one part of our incredible world. Many adults don't see the connection between cyber athletics and technology dreams. Teenagers sure do. They know how many cool things are out there right now. They also know how many more amazing things are just around the corner. For these young people with creative minds, the future is wide open. They will get college educations and bring their dreams to their careers. Their lives will be like a fantastic journey—a journey that is beautiful, fun, and unlimited . . . just like cyberspace itself.

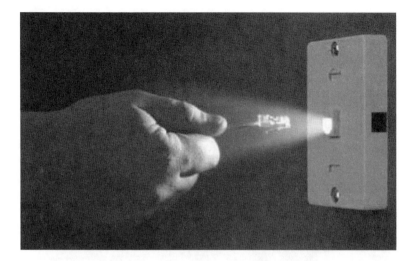

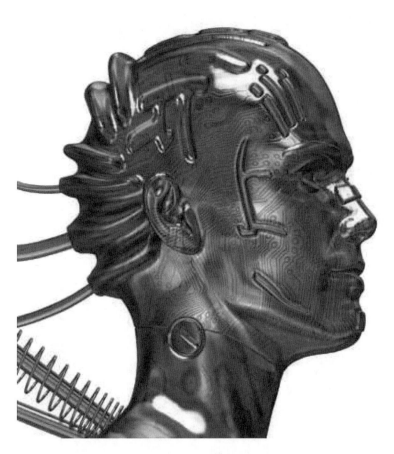

Plug in to your dreams.